EGYPT FROM SPACE

EGYPT FROM SPACE

Beckian Fritz Goldberg

Oberlin College Press
Oberlin, Ohio

The FIELD Poetry Series, vol. 30
Oberlin College Press, 50 N. Professor Street, Oberlin, OH 44074
www.oberlin.edu/ocpress

Cover and book design: Steve Farkas
Cover photograph courtesy of Image Science and Analysis
Laboratory, NASA Johnson Space Center.
(Image ISS025-E-9858, http://eol.jsc.nasa.gov/.)

Library of Congress Cataloging-in-Publication Data

Goldberg, Beckian Fritz, 1954-
  [Poems. Selections]
  Egypt from Space / Beckian Fritz Goldberg.
     pages cm. — (FIELD Poetry Series ; vol. 30)
  Poems.
  ISBN 978-0-932440-38-9 (paperback : alk. paper) —
  ISBN 0-932440-38-X (paperback : alk. paper)
  I. Title.
  PS3557.O3556E39 2013
  811'.54—dc23
                                    2012042820

Contents

distance,
O you
hand of glances

—Paul Celan

Prologue

From *Ancient Legends and Infidelities*, Ch. 12,
"The Bird That Came with Memory"

When the nightingale died the Emperor wept.

The bird that came with memory came with a schoolbus and a
ball of snow. The bird that came with memory came with a
cassia bush and a small green house. The bird that came with
memory came with a big Lincoln Continental, came with a
swimming pool. It said eucalyptus trees grow well in the desert.
The bird that came with memory came with a man named Ed.

When memory dies the bird goes on, no longer a beast of
burden. It goes on in the infinite dark you can never
contemplate without growing blank and falling back into the
world again. After memory there is no motel.

The nightingale had died neglected and alone. Its small stick
cage swinging from the pine. I could see the blue oriental
twilight sharpen each separate thing. After memory there is
now.

Say this over my death bed. All the stories you heard as a child
have become birds and migrating wolves and strange countries
which ignore tenderness, even as this delicate branch sweeps
your window.

1

I Wish I Were Mexico

When my father came back from the dead he came back as a smell. He came back as a bus passing comes back as a cloud, fumy and genie-like granting three wishes. He came back as a seaside town. He came back as the great parlor of fragrance thrown open by coconut. Meanwhile the bus was winding past Taxco, the child hanging out the window on a mountain road wanting to throw up. And when the bus turned and held itself mid-air the child died and someone else got on with her life. That's the one my father returns to because it's so simple. You breathe. And the bloom of gin comes back like a tree.

He Said Discipline Is the Highest Form of Love

All three girls were in love with their music teacher. At a lesson, he told one: You wear your heart on your sleeve. Then the other came in, dark hair parted in the middle like a black book. She had the longest most promising fingers, but he did not love her. The third girl did not come until the next day. In the night she dreamed that he spread his arms out behind her and then wrapped his left arm to hers holding the instrument, and folded her fingers so they touched the strings. His right arm crooked with her arm holding the bow. They were just one violin.

Every time she practiced after that she felt his limbs on her limbs, his breast at her back, like a man-shadow cast by her small girl body. An hour would go by like an arrow. That's what was hardest: what love did to time. The Brahms fell apart like a glass. His shoulders over her shoulders. Even when she grew up, which happened in a night, and was happy, she could still conjure him, this love skin. This whole petal of him.

When she came to her lesson the next day he tapped the lip of her music stand with a baton, tic-tic-tic, four-four time. She felt—a bit, a bit of his ankle in her ankle, and then the knee above that, floating. She wondered what he was like with the book-haired girl. She knew he loved those long fingers. Maybe that was enough. In time.

Past Immaculate

In those days every mother knew it was important to be clean, for her child to be clean, in case an accident occurred and you had to be undressed from your bloodiness by strangers, your underwear remained immaculate. The body, your body, was not allowed to speak. For when the body spoke it was foul, it was always some word like piss or fart or shit, some phrase like fucking asshole, some primitive sentence like Fuck you. And then that wretched guffaw of the puke. What a bilious vocabulary. To be clean, they knew, was to be vigilant. Bodies should be seen and not heard.

In those days, bodies knew their place and kept it and when the ambulance driver gave you up to the gurney in ER you were perfume. This is what the old men mean when they talk about the past saying, I remember when bodies were like lilacs and crisp snow. And another nodding, And quiet, so quiet a ghost might take them for a spirit. I remember, another says, an arm bright as a kitchen. And I remember, one is saying, a sex of soap roses. A regret as hard as bleach.

From *Ancient Legends and Infidelities*, Ch. 3, "Perverse Muses"

> *Every poem has its pig.*
> —Rilke

The motorcycle passing my bed at night has a rumination so umbrageous the whole night stirs. And then the low endless *wwhaaaa* of cars far away. This is the whole thing: At night through the silence to hear something far away. If it is a bell, a dog, a motor, a door shut—

In the story of the princess locked in the castle every night she'd listen for the sound of a key, for every night someone would come down the long torchlit corridor and drop their key, clink, on the stone floor. Through the space under her cell door all she could see was shadow, bending to pick up the key. Or so she imagined.

It is a great moment in a story when someone pauses at a door but does not open it.

The motorcycle disappears into its own whisper and leaves me the wake of the road, the little location I can sense just under my left shoulder a moment before it dies.

Over time she fell in love with the clumsy shadow.

The rest of the night, silent, maybe a crack in the joists, or the flicker of a bird, the wind, though there's seldom wind here. And the life of the princess may have gone on endlessly like this, except for the pig. Who was, of course, a prince with a curse on him. The jailer kept him as a pet. He kept the key chain around the pig's neck and, at night, when the pig tried to sniff under the princess's door, the key clinked against the stone. The pig, you see, was a terrible voyeur of fragrance and he thought he smelled a truffle in there.

And so the things that pass are not, after all, what we think they are. Meeting them face to face won't save us. What saves us is the bed we make for ourselves in the bodies we can't bring out of the dark. What saves us is the love we think they would have for us if each minute did not have its own direction.

Egypt from Space II

Last night from one peak in the Rockies I could see the Nile. It was distant enough to seem still. That blue of nightsky before stars. It was only in the morning I knew geography had had me. And not the first time. And not the only thing. I had seen the cat, once, swimming easily in the glittering ocean, arriving with the shells. Both were joys—unreal, transient, an illusion. But I remember these as well as I remember the solid and constant, the bed I sleep on. The river—the snake that followed my window to the edge and lay shimmering. I was deep in the book of the house and did not hear it calling.

Faithful

A man had lived with the body of his wife in their trailer for eleven years, and then one day had enough and walked to the police station and confessed. He had not killed her, he insisted. It was just that one day, eleven years ago, he'd come home and she was dead and he didn't know what to do. He made supper. Beans and onions with a little leftover chicken. After that it was television and sleep and, in the morning, breakfast. He went on being normal, was that a sin? He did not know how to acknowledge that life was loss, that he had lost, that nothing would ever be the same. His neighbors went to work, came home, petted their dogs. There were bicycles laid down in driveways. Who wanted to turn away from such peace. Even the stink became a habit after a while, imagine a church where the incense was human. Imagine a religion where denying everything was salvation. Imagine the double-wide, the little nails in the vinyl on the front step, and the rusted metal roadrunner propped against the front. Does it look like a house death would choose? Does it look like a house where the hand of God would reach down and wrench out your heart the only mercy that he let you look away?

Far Demon Apple Body

—for Chico

The silver of the bite runs down your chin. But this was the end
of the story. Where the juice is. Was, all along. Your mouth
snapped off an hour from the clock. The clock was running.
Which reminds me: the story had a dog in it, an erotically ugly
stink of a little dog. It had lived near the railroad tracks. It had
once eaten a child. You let it sleep on your sheets. Pant near
your head. You think of how a breath runs at night. Your life is
nothing but a sweet instruction you must disobey. A dog is a
great help. How he takes his tongue to himself and an hour
passes.

Bedtime Story

The way I can carry a canary on my finger through the house, you'd think the littlest part of my body was a light somewhere else. I have been able to do this since I was a child. Since I was a child the boat on my head and the whistle in my hip have both fallen and disappeared. They say it's important for a woman to have balance. She needs balance in order to have grace. That way the boat and the pale white pear don't get lost. And the plunger neither. The way I can carry pitch black on my lips, the way I can carry a gun in my sleep, the way I can carry bottles all stacked up my spine and a backgammon piece in my ear and the whole gulf of Aqaba on my perfume, you'd say I was a body on a spirit and spirit's looking precarious. Even now someone next to you may be carrying on his shoulder, a side of beef or an astrolabe. You never know who's carrying an 1/8" screwdriver in their gut. Look closely. At the body: a place from which thing after thing has fallen. The way I can carry the book of sitting. The way I can carry the book of kneeling. And the way I can carry the book of leafing through over and over. Carrying the farmhouse and the chickens and dad's clarinet and this desert and the fine night and the TV-murmur and your sleep all at once—they say it can't be done. You can't carry the gray roof and the wire coop and the black velvet-lined case and the saguaros and the 5th of November and the boy in the late movie saying he's going to make more trees…not without dropping a pear or a gun. And it may be true. Sometimes I sway, and men throw down their pillows. A child carries his bedtime all through his life.

Intermittent Rose Body

They took the heart into the baboon. Into the neck. It was a pig heart and it made minutes. The thirteenth day the baboon sat with his hand on his heart and they noted, *baboon walks with his hand clamped to his neck.* It began to ooze, this wound that wasn't a heart's, wasn't a neck's, but was progress. It wasn't life and it wasn't myth. As when memory gives someone a rose. Baboon X201 survived thirty-one days and his heart stopped. The pig stopped. They noted the time, because time had left the body. The blood stood in folds. It was an anniversary of sorts without romance without take me in your arms.

Red Car I

I follow you sleek red car that dream crashed into a rack of
dresses at the bottom of the hill, struck and swaying like female
ghosts. Heartbeat, I follow you, even your exhausted ghost
glistens like pomade, and I arrive at the coffee house just in time
to catch you peeling from the windowlight and buzzing like a
mind to the road out of town. Cherry Bomb, I follow you,
watery with desire, past the horse factory where I work, the
bread station and the warehouse liquors. They slip past my face
like sequined fish, the speed of my desire so marine, so liquid,
though many think water is slow as air is quick. It's just that we
lose time there and even there the red car has the undulation of
a sting ray which is the red car in a heat mirage. You must follow
me: We are after the red car which is now cruising the bedroom
neighborhoods as I squint across the lawn and feel my house, the
next, slide by, its bright mirrors, its guttural croon, the red car
suddenly guns like blood for air and gone—

Wigs Amor

When I passed the window sign *Wigs Amor* I wanted to know
just what love was wearing these days. I wanted to know where
the men who were women were tonight, shaved and platinum,
as morose as they were gay—and who had his eye on the
mannequin with ringlets?

That this should be a business, both lucrative and prosthetic.
That there should be a sign proclaiming the cupidity of hair.

That there should be a woman inside, brunette for today,
Hungarian and plump forever, carrying an audacious red bob
toward the pale bald girl seated at the mirror. But this would not
be *amor*. —I hate it, said the girl.
—A little make-up..., said the Hungarian.
—It's not what I look like.
—What do you want to look like.
—Like me, the girl said, I want to look like me. Not like some
cancer poster-whore.

They went through Theda Bara, Marilyn, Morticia and Rita.
They went through Lucy and Lady Godiva, Veronica and Evita,
Heidi and Bowie.

At the end of the day there was a pale hill of hair on the floor,
and all along the counter, falls of chestnut, auburn, ash brown
and black. The head-mannequins were like large naked alien
eggs lining the shelves. And with the pale sickly bald girl, chin
on her hand in the mirror and in the window, the Hungarian,
wigless now but for a few wisps with bobby pins, behind the girl in
the mirror and the window, someone was looking lovestruck, I
swear, among all that drag of emptiness and long dark swimming.

Boywatching with Lydia

Sharks, you think, looking out to the distance where they float in their school, those boys in their wetsuits sitting on their boards waiting. The boards drift in place like petals until the boys rise up black, holding the center and ride into the curl before the white crest wilts and falls. Meanwhile the lull is great. The cloud cover thickens. Later in the beach parking lot they peel back into their white and brown bodies, beautiful and sequential as time-lapse lilies, and that one freckled shakes out his hair while they talk among themselves in their easy, disposable language. And that one, waist deep in his shadow, goosebumped as the breeze blows a kiss to each nipple. I watch them carefully now—flowers, not fish, now that they're close enough to know I'm watching. And I know how it looks. The long boards leaning like shields against the dull blue truck and the towels like hours draped around their necks. Waiting is everything. Just you wait and see.

2

Red Monsoon

The lipstick, a lowdown slinking hound of a red, the lie of *I was at home alone*, a low slung hip-swing of red, a full velvet-vulvaed red hibiscus in the dewlight, and sudden as blood. With its soft point and its flat cheek, the lipstick pressed into the bow of her upper lip and followed it to the corner like a smooth dance dip. She liked the red coming on to her. Then the kiss of her upper and lower lips to each other and the brief puff of their parting. Oh, to draw on an eye like this, or a nipple. Or another flesh. To glow like perfect alibi. To sex the simple black dress. Red hugging the curve, and the lips in their eloquent waxing, the woman-bird knows the power of a wound this fresh and just for the occasion.

Galaxy Coffee Shop

Like women who carry candies in the zippered compartment or the smile of a patent leather after the magnetic click of the purse, the mirage around the next curve of highway—it moves as you move and stays exactly ahead. In the Chinese restaurant in Yuma, the waiter will serve both you and Dad enormous vodka gimlets though you are twelve. You are sure you look mature for your age. This is the year your father's in the janitorial business. You eat beneath the Galaxy Coffee Shop's sparkling roof in Gila Bend, you stay at the same main drag hotel in Yuma happy with a pool and TV, wrapped soaps and shampoo bottles that fit in your palm. One night you write a letter and tape it to the inside of the lampshade so when the lamp is switched on the writing shows. Later, two guys stay there in the room and write you back. You don't know what to do. You drink lime slush and eat fried chicken. You gaze out the car window at the dunes, smooth as if time had never come here. But there is a translucent curl of heat above them, an occasional shimmer that follows beside the car. One night at the bar near the base an air force man asks you to dance and Dad says OK and you had never been held so close and felt so miserable. And the misery was secret. You are sure you look sad for your age. There is the pool at night warm as a bath and the television bolted to the wall, blessing the bed, the occasional thunk and rumble of the ice machine down the corridor. On the ride home you eat at the hamburger stand on Highway 60 and gas up at the Mobil. The sky cloudless and an endless even blue you never get to though later you put your finger in the steakhouse table's candleflame fluttering from its plastic-netted red glass. While he's in the Men's you enjoy the underworld of adult faces, the highlight of their chins, the way the shadows hit a cheek, then plumb the pale clavicle of the fiftyish lady in the tight crimson dress. You are sure she should appear in your autobiography which you are working on now as you have been from childhood and paying attention which is the pleasure of itself.

Hothouse No. 7

As a man with one ball is a monorchid, there's a flower made
completely of four-year-old girls' nipples, that pink with the
white still in it. But that is nothing next to the giant corpseflower
filling the air with decomp. In Latin, *Amorphophallus titanium*.
Men flock for miles just to see it, the way that form sometimes
defies function. Especially in this heat, this tropical mist, as the
passionflower vine has painted all its eyelashes and put golden
earrings through the delicate purple foreskins that we might
follow them somewhere dark like the roots hanging from the
peat. As a close summer just before thunder—and the lightning
changes sex, suddenly, like a zipper. Into feeling.

Hillside

Each sadness is alone in us like a gown fallen inside the bride, a flower collapsed inside the groom. They had not been married long and they were not happy, and they knew no reason why and he, sometimes, cupped his hand against the heavy black wing of her hair as she looked away. She had eyes that weighed as much as temple bells.

The feeling was a kind of tolling. You've felt it when someone beside you was hiding desire. Hiding an ocean. Kneeling the unspoken.

Desire was in this pair of sadnesses, too. It was the point in the story where heart eats plot, and denouement is everything.

When she looked away there were white leaves like coins over the pond. And then we were in a kitchen. Or I was, watching them in the next room. Several things: a piece of iron running from me to him, silk cherry blossoms staring like snow above the table, a sneak geography from our other lives, that hillside…

As sure as memory steals, dream stacks love against us.

From *Ancient Legends and Infidelities*, Ch. 2, "Sexual Shamans"

It was a fact the Sultana Bird could walk on water even when there weren't floating plants. It could run across the marsh without sinking and when it did it appeared as an iridescence, a beaming hyacinthine streak. Then it would disappear off the map which was made of water vapor because the country was too slow, too insecure about its borders and the people there uncertain to a definite degree. What mattered was they made the effort over a period of time, to cultivate a belief. It didn't have to be a large one like life after death or the earth circling the sun. But just one belief in something else. The day the appliance repairman slept with the glazier's wife, someone passed the window glowing purple and called the glazier. After he slashed the man's buttocks with a shard he told everyone it had been the Sultana Bird who detected the adultery, just as the ancients said. Then there was a lot of handshaking and belief all around. Because sometimes a true story becomes true overnight, the way something someone said you hated long ago suddenly blooms through a quiet supper, the sun just down, the sky wine above water.

She Said It As If She Were Milk

Tonight I shall rewrite the Odyssey. I love the word complimen-
tary, she said, almost as much as a pig loves dress up. She said it
as if she were milk. Penelope was dressed for the rodeo. Here
see a footnote in the original Greek which wildly translates says,
"Some say the name Homer is a corruption of the Greek word
for chambermaid, pronounced *chammer* with the German
gutteral 'ch,' and in Greek spelled: *Haeoeoeotheologolopis*, with the
emphasis on the 'o.'" Penelope's python sandals almost seemed
to sparkle big as her belt buckle. She was as cute as Texas and
lonely as Troy. She took up weaving and tonight, while rewriting
the Odyssey, I became lonely for my ship, whatever ship that
might be. And I began to think of the names of ships: Wind
Mistress, Imagine, Hi Ho Silver, Briny Marlin, Dauntless, Karen
Marie, Irish Luck. My Alibi, Happy At Last, Prowler, Libra,
Bluebell, Blue Star, Brown Eyes, Second Chance. The Other
Woman, My Girl, Fancy Free, and Equinox and Restless and
High Time…. In my odyssey only the pigs come home, pinkish
improbable beasts. The house goes to ruin if not rack, the pigs
run all over the house snouts to the ground recognizing nothing,
like pigs at sea, and broody Telemachus at the loom drinking
cups of red wine till the threads go sailing. I just *love* how all you
ever think about is murder, she said, and every bit as much as a
beet loves red. *Dreamer, Sea Lion, Sunray, Wayward Angel.* She had
fringe everywhere. Her eyes were aquariums. Two people
longing for different things may long them together. Second
footnote.

Egypt from Space I

—for C. W.

Whatever the landscape is, shadow crushes into the rocky places and the light is plunged with forms down to the violet needletip of the barrel cactus, and the short dark saucer beneath the hopscotching wren, like a little drip pan under him wherever he goes—though here, in the desert, there are no shadows for several months a year. After the first month, we do not even remember them. Our windows turn to mirrors. It hardly pays to leave the house, too hot out there to feel your breath. The lizards sleep vertically on the walls, like puppet arabesques.

We stay inside and run the air into the deep pink evenings, pangs of gold then the blue litmus and the creosote bush crazing into silhouette against it. We have not figured out the meaning, but have learned to stand still for this. Blade-drop of night. The resinous odor. The desert belongs to space and the moon, a white thumbpick tonight, enough to see the ridge of the mountain has remained a cabal of dull brown skulls.

By autumn the shadows draw what they see lying down. The curved limbs of the paloverde and the stipple of its veil—a Nile river delta, its albedo backscatter of birds from the distant photosatellite.... Whatever the landscape is we want its memory, much longer than ours, never leaving its body.

Red Car II

But I traced the roads until they led to you flashing by the
downtown jeweler's and then slipping the corner. You were so
far then I had to have you, hot machine—that you were not
human made you more dream, much as the newly dead are,
burning off memory palms first mouth first eyes first. When
you are away I am jealous for your life—strut and piston, road
and radion, pedal and valve and shield—as I am now of the
sun starting down the other side of the mountain, shadow
whooshing toward the house. Each night it sets a new record, I
think, until my last days might be fast enough to almost—
almost—touch you, though you throb once in the corner
streetlight. Late, I stand sleepless gazing out toward the
memory I left in the middle of geography once when I spotted
you on the 10-South to Tucson and had to repeat a whole year.

December 28 as Part of the Body

A lapse into rain and the pale bark glows like fat, Mormon tea bush, Indian tobacco, turpentine bush, the bristling cholla. The javelinas walk from the wash with their stiff mohawks and long noses, in the softest drizzle of winter, ignoring my house, turning those faces rough as hemp and not seeing me. In the game of human and animal they get points for this, the gaze that says, *you are not here, you are of no substance in this world.* The human, then, falls back. December 28, the rain suspended now, a flood of light and thorns bright as nipples. No one ascribes a soul to the day which also lives and dies. As if time had no life but ours.

A View of Popocatepetl

When my father died again, again I was too late. The eyes had
bloomed already into their stare and his body had become the
cat's, unreasonable and soft, the way one death gets confused
with another—one childhood with many other and older
strangers, like the one who leaned over a long time ago and put
his fist through the door of the bedroom. Geography began to
wander the house.

There, mother was pointing to the mountain topped with snow,
See how it looks like a sleeping lady? The hotel pool in Mexico
clogged with purple bougainvillea petals drifting from the
patio, and I so young again, a fat *camerera* had to strike one to
light my breath.

Poem with Competing Theories of Pomegranate

My darling sweet red honeycomb, my little boat of water rubies, my little blood-drops-for-the-navel, heed my tongue. You came from the rib of the red moon which was meant to orbit the other world, the stained world.

What shit. The pomegranate was once a potato. It is a mutation.

And everyone hears these two voices whether they acknowledge them or not, for everyone knows into red goes beauty as into a glove a hand. Knows form lies with form and color with color, that to bell is to hollow, that to darken is to come close.

Everyone hears his past and his present all at once, his desire and his not at the same moment, the flutter within the circle. Sweet, sweet blister after blister, gleam after gleam, red fog on the panes...

Everyone looks for a pair of soft eyes in all those faces.

Art and Life

In October the artist began painting a woman in front of a
boutique. Day by day her dress began to fill in, and her
green-gold buttons, then her toes filled in her white sandals by
mid-month, the beads on the sandals, blue, red, yellow. Before
dinner, the wife would come upstairs to his studio and look
over the day's progress. "What did I do today?" he'd ask her.
The feet, she'd say. Or, The mannequins in the window, she'd
say. Sometimes she'd look a long time and then say hesitantly,
The sky? Other times, it was instantaneous. She'd arrive on the
top step of the stair and exclaim, The breasts! On those
occasions the evening would go well.

By Halloween the painting was nearly done, the woman's
bleached blonde hair, the ruffles around the buttons, the shadow
in the sternal mastoid and the dot of light near the center of each
eye. What did I do today? She frowned a while. The forehead?
—No, no. Look.
—The chin?
—The nose, he said, how do you like the nose?
She hesitated. The nose looked like a little smashed butternut
squash.

And so November went. Each night he would have her come
up and look at the nose.
—How is it now? And she'd nod. And he'd get angry and tell
her to go fuck herself what did she know about noses.

The next night he had her come up and look and she failed to
appreciate the little white highlight he'd put on the tip. The
next night she failed to appreciate he'd moved the highlight left.
And so on. All through November and December he narrowed
the bridge, he shrank the nostrils, he widened them, he made

the nose more wedge-shaped, more aquiline, shorter, longer. It looked like a two-headed worm. It looked like a baklava. He and the wife were no longer speaking. She refused to come out of her room.

Eventually the man grew lonely with nothing but a nose for company and painted a pretty red rose right between the woman's eyes in a final homage to the olfactory organ. Please, please come up, he begged the wife. Slowly and mistrustfully, and smelling a little musty, the wife came up the stairs and exclaimed, "The rose!" though it looked more like a hemorrhage, and once more there was harmony between art and life.

Red Car III

Red car, with the gleam of a showroom everywhere you go. I
was a little girl when I first saw you. Love was in the detail, red
swoop, flames down to your fins, I loved that you were not
animal but alive as the butcher bird or the sinfish. Transit,
that's what dazzled, and I fell *in transit,* as if I were the shy
roadside gravelghost in your speed nor was there time then to
climb in, to imagine the ten thousand revolutions toward the
red zone. I followed you for thrill, blood's car, thrill of a child
as it gets later, later, afraid she might be caught. That spring
night she began to believe she could telepath desire, move
objects with her mind. That spring I made the schoolroom
clock dance in the room, the spoon rise above the table, until I
saw you, red car, clear the bridge over the town's artificial lake
and stayed on you as far as the Desert Postcard Museum before
my life resumed and I'd gone too long without sleep.

The Rose I Send Myself

That rose is as sad as leaving the beach. Blowsy and sagging.
All towels. The whole world is suddenly dogless. In this way
sadness is the most particular.

Things to do when a rose comes up from nowhere: call your
mother, mourn, admit it, don't, and step out in the cool night.
It can be a stranger's face. A scent. It comes up like a thought
you don't know you're having until it's between your teeth.

Dancing ensues. The first pink dips the water. The rose is
attached to no other memory, it is alone. That's why it must
belong to childhood. It must be something I kept to myself.

The end of summer, lipstick long on the napkin. To be humble
and surrender is all it thinks about, that rose. All head. The last
umbrella stuck in the sand.

An image can ruin you. An image can doom you. The eye's
much bigger than the heart. Why pretend memory has
something to teach us, that wilting evangelist...

3

Story Problem

If Keisha had three million pears and a trainload of apples left
Cleveland at 64 miles per hour and on it was a man who had
lost one wife and two dogs in his current lifetime at 64 miles per
hour approaching Euclid then Ashtabula, the lake wind
shimmying and the compartment windows and each car having
ten compartments how much of a wonder is it when asked to
care about all this we fell asleep, we dreamed that love is a form
that comes for us, after Ashtabula, after Conneaut. How many
pears does Keisha want? And what if sometimes in our dreams
people changed as Keisha in the future will be Keith. And if
somehow, by the time the train pulls into Erie, three and one-
half apples have disappeared, what of the water, what of the
wind, what of the two dogs, the one wife. What kind of life is it.
A. The man's name is Charlie. B. The pears are Anjou. C. There
is nothing after Ohio. D. A and C. E. All of the Above. F. None
of the Above. Gee, we hope that Keith gets married and has a
normal life. We hope the dogs are in dog-heaven. Though we're
only partially awake. And if at the same time the apples left, a
child woke up in the dark of Lorain like a leaf, hearing the hush
at 6 miles per hour, which would stop breathing first? This is at
last the essence of the problem as sure as a gardenia. Which had
to enter this story even if through a backdoor. Though most of
us don't want to hear about a story—so think of whisky which
also has a backdoor. This then is a story about whisky. About
fermented pears. Whatever sure fires exist, and forms come to
us. We hope Charlie meets an attractive widow and gets a puppy.
We're not made to understand. The puppy is small and white
and barks a lot. The hell with Lorain. It is white, white as the
soul was invented, its ineffability dispersed into the seconds at
the rate of train windows to grass, but cute—and wriggling—
and if the dog was born on the first day of daylight savings, by
which you know how old are the apples in their train, or you
know nothing, still, after all, or ever will, take a guess. A.
Because in infinite time we will be right once.

A Veronica

When I was small I wanted a cape, how it flung itself on the air
and poured over the shoulders settling like a countryside, its
deep green wool. And the grass bent silver where the moon
looks, the shape of the wave the same as the wave's gesture,
cape made of tinier and tinier capes, each cell of my finger a
miniature finger, each cell *sol o sombra* like seats for the bullfight
that July in Madrid.

The bull was streaming with blood from the picadors &
bewildered before the matador even entered the ring with his
molecular glitter. The bull was already dying and why watch
death stumble in the wake of a veronica, its cursive scarlet over
shadow, writing only to itself, losing all romance & espionage,
losing its figure—

We forget what we once wished for, what we knew would
transform us. I was looking for the exit and wandered into a
dark place, sunlight in swords from all directions through gaps
in the boards as a man in a bloody apron butchered the body,
the head staring that way as if thinking, the smell in the warm
air of shit & wood & the meat that would be given to the poor.
I never wanted to see bravery again. But I see it now,
everywhere, that clutch of wet black rubies spilled against the
bone.

Journey

And suddenly I missed the bread we had several weeks ago,
crusty, thoughtful, like a field, and redolent, the remainder kept
on the kitchen counter for two days until it hardened and we
tossed it out. It was the field behind the house, sometimes rows
of phlox and snapdragon, sometimes alfalfa, the purple
blossoms I'd suck in my mouth for the faintest sweet, but it was
not childhood in this longing, it was bridehood, meaning I and
the absence alone.

Screamer

Let's not bring out memory's erotica, the negligées whose silk
thrills it like ice dropped right where, right where. I don't have
to say. I'll say instead there was a peacock the owners kept
behind the greenhouse at the nursery where I used to buy
flowers. Once in a while he'd scream & someone with a
geranium in each hand jumped. After the second time it wasn't
me. Take him, for example. I don't know why he still shows up
in my head spreading his iridescent emerald eyes with the
worlds in them sixteen times. It's all about holiness in numbers.
It's all a mathematical impulse on the lips & doublets of the
carmine geranium time comes up with. And why we keep
falling for what we fall for, the wary oculi looming, glowing
with an intelligence like an equation/wet with rain. That's how
the story goes when memory doesn't have its strict switch &
eloquent stilettos to give it meaning.

The Hollows

1. Gargoyle

Throat the dragon rose from the river of the body to be tamed at last by women and their amulets. So went the style of a century. Off the courtyard in the trees the birds had no throats only a little organ flinting in the dark, a spark of sound. Between head and heart, not much. These were the times dragons actually existed, a time that occurs mainly in boyhood, and briefly. From this there rose the idea of putting beaklike faces under cathedral windows and buttresses and around fountain spouts everywhere. A presence, even an ugly one, is a comfort. This is why the body has the big toe. This is why the nipple has its hairs. And fashion resuscitates form. This is why earrings. Why chokers. Every age must have its sensual member.

2. Hollows

Behind the breast, behind the fat, the grotto: retromammary
space. Behind the knee, the floating cave where the groan and
the ache live. And then the beautiful lake of the pleura caught
in its sheer sack. The flesh is not solid, it is hollows, some
occupied, some not. This is how the lizard lives in my foot.
And in the other, does not. Mostly they are dark places,
subdural mysteries where time can't be measured, not like it
can beyond, in light years, which equate vibration, duration.
These are dark years, bats, time of the blind which is from here
to *here.* Oh, when they tell you of a snakeless island or an
underworld of fire, these are just excuses. There are mothers in
trees. There are mathematical invasions. There are losses from
the very very beginning.

3. Child of Cups

Every cup must have its finger. I was a child in a room of cups
cozied on the shelves, the chinas were Meissen or Syracuse or
bone. Most had flowers on their lips and one had lips at the
bottom which stayed pursed all through the drinking of coffees
or teas. My mother was the collector of cups, the kind of
woman they bred that generation, though some preferred china
birds who lined the sills, and some china dogs named Gog and
Magog and Sandy. But I was the child of cups and couldn't
keep my finger out—I'd dip and wipe the dust from the hip of
the Royal Albert Rose cup, the saucer propped behind it on
display, admire the buttery demitasse with its gold halo and
crackled fluting, these curves to keep space in place all the
time. But one could spoil it, stick a finger in, stir, even the
pretender's sip changed history, fire into solid, solid into spent,
childhood into still-life...

Tonight I Will Execute All the Falcons of the Old Regime

About birds the surrealists were never wrong. When the drapes caught flame its wings tore the place apart. The house broke open and wet firemen walked among the charred pieces early in the morning when everything was glad to be alive. You could see their way of thinking as they stepped and the bright set of china flew over, roses on cups. Life is always impossible and why not. Sometimes the sea is the moon and the moon is the sea, and we think nothing of it. Sometimes in a dream I am sadder than I've ever been, seated on a strange couch, watching people, thinking of my father, thinking of his joy. About the phoenixes, about the iridescent tiger-winged terns, about the watch-faced sparrows, their age is about to flourish like the boot that sits up all night. The flock of buckets over the roof. In the hush by the fountain in the garden in my head, the blue Pities will alight.

Holy War

There were no bodies anymore, only parts of bodies, and few of these. Twenty-six legs in the makeshift morgue. Pieces were found even far away from the bombed places. But mostly ash. Families carried faces of their loved ones to show anyone who'd look. All day the diggers digging and they found one charred button. A man was walking in the park. He could smell the smoke from far away. The dog was bounding ahead and bounding back and bounding ahead and back the way dogs do, in love with the coming, in love with the going. There weren't many people out and a green park seemed strange these days. When the dog kept his nose down to the grass, the man looked down and there was something, and it took a moment to recognize. It was one cheek, just one cheek of a buttock. And he knelt, weak suddenly, appointed suddenly to protect this great bite from the dog.

Little Archipelago

1. Island of Cats

Gangs of cats ran in the dry old aqueducts on the island. The old man was eating at a table on the street beside the restaurant, piling shrimp shells on his plate, pale orange snarl of translucencies. During the war, he said, ships brought rats. There were no cats to kill them because the people had eaten all the dogs and cats because the island was starving. Even starving people will not eat a rat. So at the end of the war they had to bring in cats from the mainland to thin the ranks of the rodents. But there was no longer anyone who ate cat. The cats overran the port and the old city and the new streets with shops and businesses and part of the surrounding countryside. These days no one paid them much attention but to toss them an occasional scrap or shoo one away from the door. They wandered in cafes, they slept on the flat rooftops. In fact the very room in which I tried to sleep those hot August nights, the room at the top of the stairs, was directly under some communal feline boudoir. All night that horrid opera—sometimes raw and mournful, sometimes like infants in pain, and other times like persistent annoying questions…. Night after night I could hear them above me like spirits. But I did not believe in spirits, though I did believe in spirited conversation.

2. Island of Lepers

In those days, the man said, the island was home to lepers. As a boy he'd row out to the island and the lepers would wave or call out to him in his dingy and he'd wave and call back. One held his fishing pole with his armpit because most of his arm was gone.

One afternoon he saw a man rowing with a woman and a young girl toward the island. Even from a distance he could see the girl had long thick red hair that shone like copper and it made him watch her all the more as the father continued rowing toward the shore. He watched, too, as they embraced, the three of them, in that small boat and then the red-headed girl stepped onto the shore where someone was waiting to take her clothes and lead her to the disinfecting showers before she entered the colony where she would lose more and more of her body each month until the leprosy finally took her.

Now they are all empty, the showers, the roof of the small apartment house has fallen in and a large fig tree has pushed up through the center. At the top of the island beyond the old wall of a Crusader fortress is the charnel house. In the plaster wall is a square opening visitors can peer through and see the pile of bones below. There are graves nearby, shallow rectangles with thick stone lids. Most are empty now, the size of dog graves, too small for human beings.

But that day from his boat he had watched the couple row away until they shrank into the distance, the girl standing on shore, red hair fluttering like a flame, her hand raised, but still, since she had stopped waving to the dark smudge out there that was left.

Though he'd fish near the island some days he never saw the girl again, he said, until he got old. Now he sees her all the time but, he says, she still never sees me.

3. Island of Nuns

It is simply a large hill that has broken off and floated away
from the mainland, just far enough to need a boat, just far
enough so that when you were on the mainland the people on
top of the island looked tiny as birds. Centuries ago, the island
was a fortress and the great stone walls remain. Inside the walls
is a garden, abundant vines, golden ginestra, purple
bougainvillea, wild licorice, wild roses, large soft pink blossoms
with no name, honeysuckle, stalks of fleecy white and tall
black-eyed sunflowers, so overgrown that they nearly obscure
the path that leads to a bench in a stone alcove. This is a
remnant from the time the island was a nunnery occupied by
the Sisters of the Poor Clares. It was their practice, when one of
the sisters died, to seat her body on the stone bench in the
garden so that the nuns could meditate on the fragility of flesh,
the rigor, then the bloat, the rank odor, the work of maggots,
the soup of fat and organ, day after day until there was only
bone. Now a visitor may sit there where bright green lichen
cling to some of the stones, enjoying the sweet scents of
flowers and waving away the occasional bee or thought of
mortality.

Ancient Pez Cat, c. 2003 C.E.

—for Caroline

The plastic blue sphinx head with the body of a candy dispenser
is a creature from mythology even as she pulls it from her purse.
Push the head and its body drops a jaw just long enough to hold
a stack of pale orange Pez's. Then it locks back with the punch
of a pogo stick or a stapler. These are the future's archaeological
exhibits, the glass cases of miniature laughing toilets, of lamps
that love applause, windshield hula girls, and fake dog poop and
rubber vomit. Our rubies, our scepters, our fine-boned combs.
By the most trivial and transient detail of us we will be known
as we have never been known. Not from the bowel to heart. Not
in the administrations of our fleetingness, the lifted skirts of our
surface. This will be the future site of the museum of astronomy,
the white spatter of the Pleiades or the salt of the earth.

Pink Most Desert Body

February is the nowhere of the months and in the desert it is past that—the neon sign fringing the night near spring, it blinks, *Turn-Off in Ten Mi.* I like the cloud an apocalypse pink, a lipstick both pouty and galactic cheating the mind and making body float. The sky again in the lettuce field looking up from its wet places. Buckeye. Eloy. Marana. The billboard, *Buffalo Bill's Chandelier Next Exit.* The little towns of Arizona are like the man lining up clay torsos of nudes along his back wall. Genius is in situation. The birds of the darkening shoulders spell it out.

Little Mystery

A lizard with a black collar runs out & stops to give me the eye.
I can't imagine what he sees. I am still. The August heat begins
to sting. One of us will have to move—it's desert etiquette.
Meanwhile, he does a few push-ups. Waits. Then skitters under
the parched bursage & turns the color of dry branches. It puts
things in perspective. Sometimes it's comforting to know you're
irrelevant. There should be more of that. I've been wondering
why I don't dream of the dead—have I forgotten everyone? My
dreams are mostly strangers who play my friends & we spend a
lot of time in hotels & classrooms. It's enough to make one
question magnificence which, surely, there is, and to which we
are surely witness, though we will never know why. I was saying
to my friend in the dream the other night, it's the smallest thing
that breaks the heart—I meant it breaks us because of its little
mystery. Soon you begin to see it everywhere like the color of
bark, of ash, of the animal hidden.

Red Car IV

I think the dead are supposed to appear to us in such moments
as when my friend, rushing back to his dying father, saw him
unfurl in a propane fire from the tanks a truck had spilled on the
highway. Whoosh. That was his life. So said my friend who's
never seen you blossom suddenly in the underground garage nor
wound up the levels to lose you again at the surface: Another
moon landing where the object slo-mos from the astronaut's
gloved hand and out of reach. And there you sat idling by the
shoulder of my house again while I half slept and levitated
toward the wall before we both turned over to the matter of our
present.

The American Fact

Today I learned the brain uses twenty percent of the body's oxygen. Somehow this changed my view of everything: It's true that smoking does make me dumber. No wonder I can't help believing the most American poetry is in our mouths, our easy speech, as in *don't bogart that joint my friend*—What a beautiful language. So American I can almost feel GIs riding home on the bus of my tongue. Bogart was a smoker. It's a fact, we say in American, as if fact were a reverence all its own. Is I love you a fact? If we say yes is that because it's a fact or because we believe it? What then is the difference? You see what the lack of proper oxygen has done to me, done to me—I want to get in the car and just drive. A Spaniard with hauteur once remarked *poems about driving are so American.* Windows down and miles of this desert. *Don't hog the road my friend.* On the way to Mexico there are billboards counting down the miles to the turn off where you can see Buffalo Bill's chandelier. It's a fact. And the sky so blue it's sweeter than sleep... Fuck the Spaniard, I say and I mean that as a salute to attitude. Is a salute or a kiss a fact? I am an American, I need fresh air, green trees, cold water, an electric car. I am an American, I need deer on my highway, need to say shit as often as I can. My language is a mystery with its delicate indelicates, the television's mantra *male enhancement*, while the real patriots are marching and chanting *big boner, mega-dick.* Oh, I need, I say, free medicine. People are dying, that's a fact.

4

Dog

Most things that are beautiful are red. A flower is red. A painting is something else. When you say red you don't have to say blue.

What kind of memorial should we build. Should it be stone, should it be bronze, should we carve words, should we lay flowers.

I say take a dog into your house. A dog has no country. He is brown or if he is white he is deaf. When you say dog you don't have to say soldier.

Most things are settled that way. By meaning. By bumblebee, the summer's humid field, memory that sticks for no reason. A portable explosion. You don't have to say red.

The Orient

The fan was white plastic that imitated lace, stiff ribs with intricate geometrics, clicked when the girl shook it out, clicked when she folded it. They were at a concert and the girl was opening the fan, closing it, open, open, close, until a man's big hand squeezed right over hers, wrenched the fan away and broke it—like that—over his knee.

It had come from a museum shop. With the fan in front of her face her eyes could peek out at anyone. She could see through snow. She could steal glances, the favorite concubine of the Japanese emperor. But that was over now. The two pieces were still in his fist, resting on his brown trousers. The girl began to pull at her socks. From here on, memory would have no proportion to experience. The fancrusher had seen to that. Even from far away, far away, the heart remembers where it sat with thieves…

Go Away

I hate bald kids with cancer. And those Nicaraguan children
held in the arms of their bearded white Christian benefactor.
They like to smile at the TV, though they don't have, they have
seen. His jacket is khaki. My television is in the corner of the
room. Mostly it likes detectives. Jesus Christ I hate my job. But
right now someone's being arrested and sooner or later it's all
ballistics. I betray myself and tell the cat who is licking his tail
held in his paw. Then brushing his face, cleaning his claws with
his teeth. It's pure meditation. I reached that state walking
drunk from a dive bar in downtown east LA and the brother
came up to me for a handout saying he was *residentially
challenged* and I had to respect that and gave him my last
twenty. What the fuck, my dear Buddha, Vishnu, Void. And
thank Saint Someone that we found the parking garage.
Closed. So we had to pound on windows, doors. But we got
out.

Each night the bald girl's mother whispers in her ear *Go away*.
She wants to speak to cancer. She has the ear of death unlike
us lucky ones. I heard that hearing was the last sense to die and
wondered if I'd spoken to my father's body, would, would
happen. Oh, mortal fucking grammar.

The bald girl was ten and had never known anything but dying.
Her adult teeth are still coming in. She's not cute, she's not
pretty. If she were old no one would give. Who the hell is
childhood? Were we so valuable? Brave.

Red Car V

Sequin, red car, you give it to me give it to me everywhere I look
you're the movie, the earrings in the gumball machine, red as if
you cut right into sensation. The violence here is in intention,
long before I fell for your pick-up and your thrust. The object is
lush. It shines on us. It is amen. Red car, slide on like a smile
and beam. You go up in sexfire in my dreams. But I have you in
not having you. Isn't that a salesman's slogan of desire? Then
everywhere I begin to see myself stealing you, slipping in behind
the wheel, the mountains smearing past the curve before
oblivion, but oblivion's a town where I start over, imagining I've
stolen you and feel you in my blood. Your pump and pomp.

Glow-in-the-Dark Gecko

He nearly burns from the lightbulb where I make him gather
light. Along his belly is a little seam of the plastic mold he came
from, full of strontium aluminate. He is light green and
bendable. At night in the windowsill he is the extraterrestrial—
signaling out? peering in? The glow could go either way.

That somewhere there is an entire factory devoted to keeping its
eye out for a possible shortage of phosphorescent geckos.

I like to imagine that factory in Mexico, run by an old man with
a long toenail that had begun to curl as it extended as far as a
tongue.

I like to visit Tuesday nights when they run the tests.

Tonight I inspect the tail with its rubbery perfect taper. Which I
picked up first from the floor of a bar some nights ago as if it were
a dollar someone had lost and I wasn't asking what a simple
gumball machine gecko like he was doing in a dump like this.

I like to think of children sticking lit matches to the grass
clippings in suburban alleys.

As Lao Tso said to Li Tsu: Sometimes quirk is all.

The One with the Darkest Hair

The one with the plums in it. The one with the white dress. The one with the laughing monkeys and the twist-off top. The one with the sky. The one with the man and the woman and the man dies. The one with a knife in it. The one with a doll floating out to sea and the one with no dog. The one with father still in it, with silky gin in it, with the perfume of acacias in it. The one with the nails in it. The one with the man and the woman and the woman leaves. The one with the swimming pool. The one with a wasp in it. The one with the duck riding a bicycle in it. The one with holes in it. The one with the desert highway and the dark stutter of lupine in it. The one with our lips in it. Oh, the one with wood nymphs and Greek wine in it. The one with glitter in it. The one with the man and the woman and the man is killed. The one with the most moons in it. The one with forgetting in it, and pink cotton gloves. The one with the darkest hair. The one with a Cadillac and James Brown in it. The one with the yowl in it. The one with the man and the woman and the child dies. The one with sand in it. The one with two graveyard rabbits grazing. The one with the names in it and the one with the numbers in it. The one with your eyes in it. The one with your beautiful chestnut. The one. The one. The one. The one with the silver legs. The one with creosote after rain in it. The one with cat's paws. The one with the woman alone in it. The one with fresh sheets. The one with father's ashes in it. The one with the boxes. The one with the ugly doorbell. The one with the lake in it and the cloud in the lake. The one with the dog running home in it. The only one.

On the Author

What I meant was winter is most desert. Desert as a state of
space. And I never meant to write so much about the desert.
But then, as the desert says, The tree in the desert says nothing
because it has much to tell about nothing. This is a proverb. A
proverb as a state. But I never meant to talk so much about
language which is a tree in the desert. You feel it more than see
it, you know, like cloudcover in the night, or like a lawn on TV.
On TV someone almost always is having an argument. About
is a state, too. We are there. What I meant was to write about.
And then the desert spread before me.

L'Art Brut

The moon tonight is a lit canoe shrouded in a curl of mist. The
men at the bar aren't buying this. The moon is a housewife's
fingernail. Drink to the moon as the arc of a woman on top.
All shit about the moon is shit. The moon is the light pelvis of
a girl dusted of earth. Forensic moon. Moon of the Observer. I
am sorry to see it, night after night, scar in the blue skin of the
desert. Oh, yes, the day that is so blue, the night that is so
underblue. The men at the bar aren't buying. They want to hear
about the moon's tits. They were, I say, pink top hats spun
upon the alps. *Looks more like a canoe*, they say. And Dog
clambers asaintly up.

Red Car VI

It licked away this black space into the bloom which was the shadow of the red car. It thrust into the thoughtful center of noise. It slowed from the purple undone mountains. We were beginning: the brave unutterable acceleration, the profanity of truthtelling, the soft cloud left above the vanishing point. Its speed the wind where your skin was erased, wings sure especially behind the curves. It went, a meteor down the white line along this black space. It went, a bright wound after the rabbit. Salve wound, "a swan on the wound…" (Char). The intervals of time don't matter. Only its ruby solitaire and fins. The night moth at the headlight. Sometimes late at night the coyotes laugh hysterically and a rabbit is dead. Red car, my heart had all the way to the sky.

Afterlife

Casper the friendly ghost at a window looks out at the snow. A cat the size of a bear is sleeping on the dresser. Oh. It is a bear and the bear is a ghost too. Casper goes to sleep in a dresser drawer. He doesn't like to scare people. "I'm a friendly ghost."

Ghost Bear wears a yellow bow tie. His name is Harry and he shakes his belly like Santa.

The mice in the house are not ghosts. The sign outside their mousehole says CONDEMNED.

I have not seen Casper since I was seven or eight. I am surprised at the timbre of his voice, sugary and boy-like. Annoying. But I had loved him as a kid. I sang along with the theme song. And now, because of the cartoon on TV, which is a rerun, it's my child-self in rerun. Watching the cartoon I'm watching for clues to my self, who I was, what I liked, why.

When I recognized him at first I was happy because I'd forgotten. But I remembered there was a time—it must have been a regular time—I'd sit down and wait for Casper to come on. I didn't ask questions. Why the mice are alive. Why a bear needs a bow tie. Why Casper sounds like a eunuch. And why has the mousehole been condemned.

Flickering there in black and white, Casper's no more than a floating sheet. A simple ghost. He was comforting to a child who never once seemed to realize Casper had to have been someone's ghost, someone dead. I thought it sad the people, the cartoon people, he scared. He only wanted to be loved and I was the kind of child who rooted for him.

Snow looking at snow, really, a ghost in the window in the TV in the living room in my head.

Casper is in 1962. Still. Casper and Harry are both transparent against the night sky when they go flying over the houses. I see through Harry the constellation of the Dipper. Stars. I wonder about physics. How can Casper land on a branch when he passes through solid walls? When is he a cloud and when is he a sheet over a broomstick. I wondered why does a ghost need to blink.

I wondered who had died and become a friendly ghost. I cannot remember 1962.

If Casper is a ghost and transparent before the stars
If snowflakes are like stars it stands to reason

Therefore impossible to tell if the snow falls in Casper as it falls
     on him
Or, if it is Casper in the air, Casper falling
but more slowly than the snow is snowing

It is impossible to be who you were. When I picture the child she is empty. I see the glowing picture through her. The full name of the bear is Harry Carry which now I realize is a play on *hari kari*, ritual suicide. What kind of child's ghost was he, an old suicide hanging around with a young dead boy?

And yet I was glad to see him. I had not believed in ghosts even as a child. I knew they were not real. Now, she is not real. The child's not real. Yet the ghosts sail over the neighborhood as if then were now. The ghosts come to a body and sail through.

The Passing House

The way cat fur comes in cool from the night. The way you pour on your hand the white flour kept in the fridge. If coolness could be powder. If our atoms were infinite beings. And now the smallest things are so important, especially when your heart is broken as it is by the white. Imagine if the downy moon rose tonight and, while the husbands slept, you finally got to think. And that thinking, of course, involved a lifetime and its three seconds of your skin thrilling against the damp swimsuit. Chilled rose petals at the florist's shop. You felt them between your fingers. Your skin was luck. It proved whatever dies in true love can be found living elsewhere, in woven cotton or in a sudden pocket of November chill or in the hum of a mysterious machine at night. And not by the way of compensation only but as a little thunder far away is comforting when you listen from your bed. Or as the aroma of hickory smoke can be years ago in the morning in Thebes, Montana, coming from a passing house.

My Descent

Furtively my father would slip a hand under the table and knock. I was three so I'd look around and look under the table wanting to know where it came from and how and that's when father would drink my milk. I'd sit back up to a drained glass. What happened to my milk? My father would tell me it was the little girls who lived under the floor. They were hungry and wanted my milk. They might want my peas. I knew enough to sense it was a game, to half-believe there weren't really girls living below us. But I had a vision of them anyway, all blonde with long straight hair, dressed in chambray smocks with frilled white aprons, reaching up, up toward my floor. Otherwise, they seemed to accept their world which must be dark and musty. They'd knock. A chicken wing would disappear.

Invisible

In music we hear between beginning and end, the lasting. It is sorrowful stuff, without words. The same when you gaze on a royal doe or buck kneeling at rest in the heap of fallen leaves. Eternity is small and invisible like the atom.

My mother danced in front of a mirror when I was in her belly and the gaze rubbed off on me.

First, I was like a little camera. Gradually I became more human, until the camera was just an ache in my shoulder, like a violin.

Every word is true. I played Telemann and Schubert. Every note had its time and vanished.

I am sure it was a doe nesting in the brown leaves when we walked the woods and stopped still. Tiptoed down to the river.

I want this to be the omission in the story of my life.

Acknowledgments

Blackbird: "He Said Discipline Is the Highest Form of Love," "Past Immaculate"

Connotations: "The One with the Darkest Hair"

FIELD: "Bedtime Story," "From *Ancient Legends and Infidelities*, Ch. 3, 'Perverse Muses,'" "Glow-in-the-Dark Gecko," "Red Monsoon"

Gulf Coast: "Dog"

Hayden's Ferry Review: "Egypt From Space II," "Far Demon Apple Body," "I Wish I Were Mexico"

Hunger Mountain: "A View of Popocatepetl," "Egypt From Space I," "Galaxy Coffee Shop," "Hillside," "The Hollows," "Invisible," "My Descent," "On the Author"

The Indiana Review: "Intermittent Rose Body," "From *Ancient Legends and Infidelities*, Ch. 12, 'The Bird That Came with Memory'"

Luna: "She Said It As If She Were Milk," "Tonight I Will Execute the Falcons of the Old Regime"

Margie Review: "Story Problem"

Michigan Quarterly Review: "Go Away"

Mooring the Tide: "The Passing House"

Rune: "Hothouse No. 7"

Sentence: "Poem with Competing Theories of Pomegranate"

Stone Canoe: "The Rose I Send Myself"

Swink: "Boywatching With Lydia"

Willow Springs: "Art and Life," "Faithful," "From *Ancient Legends and Infidelities*, Ch. 2, 'Sexual Shamans,'" "Wigs Amor," "The American Fact"

The quotations from Paul Celan are translated by Nikolai Popov and Heather McHugh, and Michael Hamburger, respectively.